3

College Vocabulary

HOUGHTON MIFFLIN
ENGLISH FOR ACADEMIC SUCCESS

Keith S. Folse
University of Central Florida

Marcella A. Farina
University of Central Florida

SERIES EDITORS

Patricia Byrd
Joy M. Reid
Cynthia M. Schuemann

Houghton Mifflin Company
Boston   New York

Publisher: Patricia A. Coryell
Director of ESL Publishing: Susan Maguire
Senior Development Editor: Kathy Sands Boehmer
Editorial Assistant: Evangeline Bermas
Senior Project Editor: Kathryn Dinovo
Manufacturing Assistant: Karmen Chong
Senior Marketing Manager: Annamarie Rice
Marketing Assistant: Andrew Whitacre

Cover graphics: LMA Communications, Natick, Massachusetts

Photo credits: © Todd A. Gipstein/Corbis, p. 1; © Jose Luis Pelaez, Inc./Corbis, p. 18; © Tony Arruza/Corbis, p. 34; © Ariel Skelley/Corbis, p. 47; © Royalty-Free/Corbis, p. 63; © Carl and Ann Purcell/Corbis, p. 77.

Printed in the U.S.A.

Library of Congress Control Number: 2004112231

ISBN: 0-618-23026-2

123456789-EUH-08 07 06 05 04

Contents

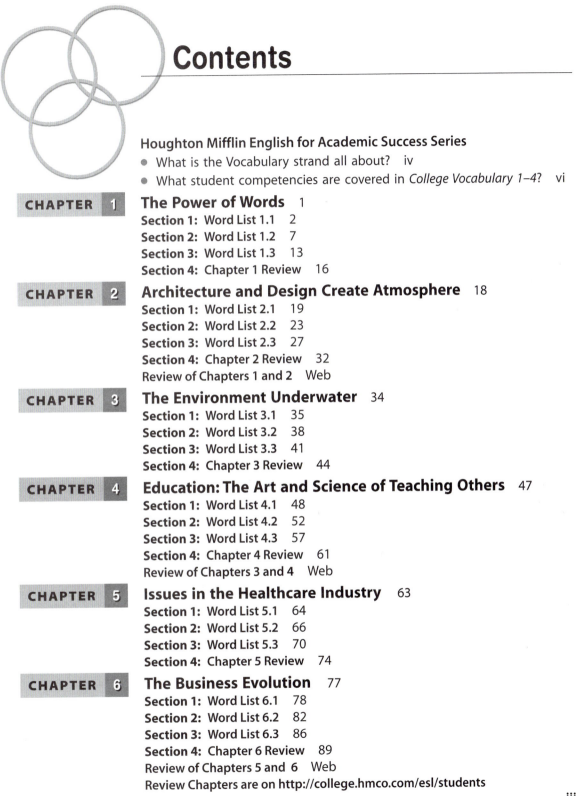

Houghton Mifflin English for Academic Success Series
- What is the Vocabulary strand all about?   iv
- What student competencies are covered in *College Vocabulary 1–4*?   vi

Houghton Mifflin English for Academic Success Series

○ What is the Vocabulary Strand All About?

The Houghton Mifflin English for Academic Success series is a comprehensive program of student and instructor materials. There are four levels of student language proficiency textbooks in three skill areas (oral communication, reading, and writing) and a supplemental vocabulary textbook at each level. Knowing how to learn and use academic vocabulary is a fundamental skill for college students. Even students with fluency in conversational English need to become effective at learning academic words for their college courses. All of the textbooks in the Houghton Mifflin English for Academic Success (EAS) series include work on vocabulary as part of academic reading, academic writing, and academic oral communication. In addition, this series provides four Vocabulary textbooks that focus on expanding student academic vocabulary and their skills as vocabulary learners. These textbooks can be used alone or can be combined with a reading, writing, or oral communication textbook. When used with one of the textbooks in the Houghton Mifflin English for Academic Success series, the vocabulary textbooks can be provided at a reduced cost and shrink-wrapped with the reading, writing, or oral communication books.

Academic vocabulary involves two kinds of words: (1) general academic vocabulary that is used in many different disciplines, and (2) highly technical words that are limited to a particular field of study. As they prepare for academic study, students need first to learn generally used academic words. A list of the general academic words called the Academic Word List (AWL) has been published by Averil Coxhead.[1] Coxhead organizes AWLs words into lists based on word families, defining a *word family* as a set of related words.

The Vocabulary textbooks prepare students for their academic study by teaching them the meanings and uses of the AWL words. The AWL word families are divided among the four textbooks with each book presenting approximately 143 word families. To see the word lists for each book, visit the website for the vocabulary series at www.college.hmco.com/esl/students.

Learning new words is more effective when words are studied in meaningful contexts. Each chapter in the Vocabulary series contextualizes a set of approximately 25–30 AWL words in a "carrier topic" of interest to students. The carrier topics are intended to make the study more interesting as well as to provide realistic contexts for the words being studied. Learning a new word means learning its meaning, pronunciation, spelling, uses, and related members of the word's family. To help students with these learning challenges, the Vocabulary textbooks provide multiple encounters with words in a wide variety of activity types.

---

1. The AWL was introduced to the TESL/TEFL world with Coxhead's *TESOL Quarterly* publication: Coxhead, A. (2000). A new academic word list. *TESOL Quarterly* 34(2); 213–238. Coxhead is also the author of the *Essentials of Teaching Academic Vocabulary*, a teacher-reference book in the Houghton Mifflin English for Academic Success series.

Each chapter has been structured to incorporate learning strategies or tips that will help students become active acquirers and collectors of words. Additionally, because research supports the idea that multiple exposures are of great significance in learning vocabulary, each word family is practiced repeatedly and many are recycled in the lessons and chapters that follow their introduction. Newly introduced vocabulary appears in **bold** type. Recycled vocabulary is indicated by a dotted underline.

Student websites for the Vocabulary textbooks provide additional practice with the AWL words as well as useful review chapters. Instructors and students can download these review chapters for use as homework or in-class study. The website for each book expands the practice with the AWL words covered in that book. Students can access vocabulary flash cards for the complete 570 word families if they choose to work with words beyond those introduced in the particular vocabulary textbook they are studying. Each of these flash cards has the AWL word, its definition, and an example.

Although, with the addition of online answer keys, this book can be an aid to self-study, it is ideally suited for classroom use. According to the focus of your course, you may choose to have your students respond to some of the exercises in writing, while you may choose to make oral activities of others. Of course, you can also incorporate practice in both skills by following oral discussion with a writing assignment. You may ask students to work individually on some exercises, while others will be better suited to pair or small-group configurations.

Acknowledgments

This book is the result of the effort and support of a wonderful group of people. we would first like to thank Susan Maguire, Houghton Mifflin Director of ESL Publishing, and Kathy Sands Boehmer, Houghton Mifflin ESL Development Editor, for their belief in and support of this series.

We would also like to thank the series editors Cynthia Schuemann, Joy Reid, and especially Patricia Byrd, whose encouragement and guidance kept us on track. We would like to thank our fellow vocabulary series authors, John Bunting, Chaudron Gille, and Julie Howard, for their experience, ideas, and friendship.

We would also like to thank our readers, Janet Biehl and Susan Reynolds, and reviewers, Meredith Massey, Mary Gawienowski, Mary Charleza, James Beaton, and Elaine Dow, for their invaluable advice and feedback.

Finally, we would like to thank family and friends for their encouragement throughout this endeavor.

○ What Student Competencies Are Covered in *College Vocabulary 1–4*?

Description of Overall Purposes

Students develop the ability to understand and use words from the Academic Word List (AWL) that are frequently encountered in college course work.

Materials in this textbook are designed with the following minimum exit objectives in mind:

Competency 1: The student will recognize the meaning of selected academic vocabulary words.

Competency 2: The student will demonstrate controlled knowledge of the meaning of selected academic vocabulary words.

Competency 3: The student will demonstrate active use of selected academic vocabulary words.

Competency 4: The student will develop and apply strategies for vocabulary learning. The student will:
a. recognize roots, affixes, and inflected forms.
b. distinguish among members of word families.
c. identify and interpret word functions.
d. recognize and manipulate appropriate collocations.
e. use contextual clues to aid understanding.
f. develop word learning resources such as flash cards and personal lists.
g. increase awareness of how words are recycled in written text and oral communication.
h. increase awareness of the benefits of rehearsal for word learning (repetition and reuse of words in multiple contexts).

Competency 5: The student will use dictionaries for vocabulary development and to distinguish among multiple meanings of a word.

Competency 6: The student will analyze words for syllable and stress patterns and use such analysis to aid in correct pronunciation.

Competency 7: The student will analyze words for spelling patterns.

Competency 8: The student will become familiar with web-based resources for learning AWL words.

The Power of Words

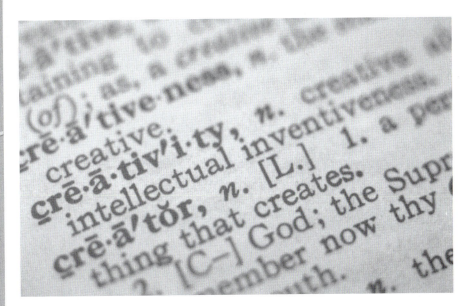

In this chapter, you will

- Become familiar with twenty-four words from the Academic Word List
- Compare *-ed* as a verb ending with *-ed* as an adjective ending
- Study the relationship between *-ate* (verb) and *-ation* (noun) forms
- Learn required preposition combinations with certain words

Section 1

EXERCISE **1** Read Word List 1.1. Then in the "Meaning/Notes" column, write a synonym or other information to help you remember the meaning of each bold vocabulary word. Use a dictionary if needed. The first one has been done for you as an example.

WORD LIST 1.1

Word	Part of speech	Example	Meaning/Notes
attributed	verb	Her success in her career can be **attributed** to her hard work and excellent language skills.	*is due to, a verb?*
detected	verb	The spell-check program **detected** several problems with your document.	
eliminate	verb	Many educators believe that increasing the literacy level of our nation will **eliminate** or at least reduce social problems such as joblessness and crime.	
identical	adjective	Homophones are pairs of words that are spelled differently but that have **identical** pronunciations.	
inspection	noun	After careful **inspection**, our instructor realized that he had spelled a word on the chalkboard incorrectly.	

Word	Part of speech	Example	Meaning/ Notes
minimized	verb	By using a simple pocket dictionary, both students and instructors who have trouble with spelling can **minimize** most basic mistakes.	
nevertheless	adverb	My mother has a very limited English vocabulary. **Nevertheless**, when she goes to the mall, she is able to communicate surprisingly well.	
revealed	verb	The book she read on the origin of languages **revealed** that many English words actually come from French.	
ultimately	adverb	Jin-A has worked hard to develop a rich vocabulary though **ultimately** it does not help her because she is shy and rarely talks with anyone.	
virtually	adverb	I once tried to memorize fifty new vocabulary words every day. I later discovered that it was **virtually** impossible to remember them all.	

EXERCISE **2**   Make a set of vocabulary flash cards to review the words in this book. Start with the words in Word List 1.1. Add new flash cards every time you study a new word list. Write each word on an index card. Then using a dictionary, write important vocabulary information on the back of each card. Include definitions, collocations (phrases where the word is commonly found), and word forms. You may also want to add pronunciation, antonyms, and grammar-related notes.

Master Student Tip

In learning vocabulary, one important aspect is repetition. Make sure you "retrieve" the meaning and form of the word multiple times. You can quiz yourself with the vocabulary flash cards in lots of ways. Here are some suggestions:
- Read the word and try to guess the meanings or parts of speech.
- Create an appropriate phrase using the new word.
- Sort the words into different categories: parts of speech, number of syllables, and so on.
- Sort the words into two groups: the ones you know immediately and with no difficulty, and the others. Then focus on reviewing the second group of flash cards until you know those words as well as the words in the first group.

EXERCISE **3**   In each row below, circle the choice that is related to the bold vocabulary word.

1. **attribute**	give the source	give the solution
2. **detect**	persuade	locate
3. **eliminate**	cut out	fill out
4. **identical**	twins	pets
5. **inspection**	a review or check	a required payment
6. **minimize**	decrease	improve
7. **nevertheless**	therefore	however
8. **revealed**	showed	enjoyed
9. **ultimately**	in the beginning	in the end
10. **virtually**	almost, nearly	often, usually

EXERCISE 4 For each sentence, underline the target vocabulary from Word List 1.1. Then circle the letter that logically completes the sentence.

1. The students' amazing reading skills can be attributed to
   a. their lack of practice.
   b. their great instructor.

2. Although not old enough to understand all the words in the newspaper article, the young children were able to detect from the photographs of burning houses that
   a. something bad had happened.
   b. something good had happened.

3. When the instructor eliminated homework for the rest of the semester, the students were
   a. happy.
   b. not happy.

4. The numeral 2 has an identical pronunciation as the word
   a. *tow.*
   b. *too.*

5. The article that Leo submitted yesterday was good. In fact, it was too good. The language was too technical and sophisticated to be original. After closer inspection, the editor concluded that the young man must
   a. have an incredible vocabulary far beyond his years.
   b. have copied it directly from a website on the Internet.

6. The grammar teacher gave each student a slightly different test to minimize the chance of
   a. copying or cheating.
   b. failing or getting too many wrong answers.

7. Some students were having trouble using the new idiomatic expression correctly. Nevertheless, because he saw that they were at least trying, the instructor
   a. felt pleased at the students' attempts to use the expression.
   b. regretted trying to teach the students any new expressions.

8. Although the flight attendant said, "You're welcome," her sarcastic tone revealed that
   a. she probably didn't mean it sincerely.
   b. she loved helping all the passengers.

9. She tried to learn all one hundred new words, but ultimately she was
   a. able to do this.
   b. unable to do this.

10. The letter combination *ng* can begin a word in some languages, but
    this is quite rare in English. In fact, there are virtually
    a. many English examples of words starting with *ng*.
    b. no English examples of words starting with *ng*.

THEME: WORD ORIGINS

EXERCISE 5   Use vocabulary words from Word List 1.1 to fill in
the blanks in this paragraph about the history of the word *sincere*. The
first one has been done for you as an example.

  Sincere comes from two Latin words: *sine* meaning "without"
and *cera* meaning "wax," but what does the current meaning
of *sincere* have to do with "not having wax"? The current meaning
of the word *sincere* can be (1) *attributed* to dishonest
merchants over two thousand years ago. In ancient Rome, people
used dishware made of clay. As you can imagine, the process of
making clay dishes and clay cups was long and difficult, and
workers were careful in making the dishware. (2) _____,
small cracks would appear in the dishware during this process from
time to time. Dishware makers who were not honest would simply
apply wax in an attempt to cover up the flaws in the products.
Because this inferior product was almost (3) _____ to
a good one, customers rarely (4) _____ any problem.
Even after a careful (5) _____ of the product, it was
(6) _____ impossible to see any problem beforehand. As
a result, customers bought the inferior product, took it home, and
used it. When the customers washed the dishware with hot water,
the wax melted, which (7) _____ the poor quality of the
dishware. (8) _____, customers came to know which
dishware merchants sold good products, products that were "sine
cera" or *sincere*. Once customers found a merchant whose products
were "without wax," they were able to (9) _____ or
perhaps even (10) _____ the possibility of buying
flawed dishware.

**Candles are
made of wax.**

Section 2

EXERCISE 6 Read Word List 1.2. Then in the "Meaning/Notes" column, write a synonym or other information to help you remember the meaning of each bold vocabulary word. Use a dictionary or use the information in Exercise 7 if you need help. The first one has been done for you as an example.

WORD LIST 1.2

Word	Part of speech	Example	Meaning/Notes
accompanied	verb	The president was **accompanied** by several professional translators on his overseas tour.	*to go with someone, keep someone company*
aid	noun	The flash cards available in the school library are a very useful **aid** for remembering word parts.	
analysis	noun	An official **analysis** of your test revealed that your highest score was on the vocabulary section. Congratulations!	
coupled	adjective	Months of cultural immersion, **coupled** with regular one-on-one tutoring sessions, often result in much faster language learning.	
enhanced	verb	Boring writing can be greatly **enhanced** by including stronger, more colorful descriptions.	
eventually	adverb	It is difficult to notice any progress at first, but **eventually** you will realize how much your skills have improved overall.	

Word	Part of speech	Example	Meaning/ Notes
normal	adjective	Forgetting newly learned vocabulary is a **normal** part of the vocabulary learning process.	
presumption	noun	After hearing her accent, the instructor made the **presumption** that she was probably Russian.	

EXERCISE 7 In each row below, circle the choice that is related to the bold vocabulary word at the left.

1. **accompanied**   alone   together

2. **aid**   assistance   comprehension

3. **analysis**   careful study   long discussion

4. **coupled**   one thing   two or more things

5. **enhanced**   better   worse

6. **eventually**   at some time before at some time after

7. **normal**   usual   special

8. **presumption**   a supposed belief   a mistaken identity

COUPLE

The word *couple* has several forms with different meanings, but all these meanings are related to "connect" or "be together." Consider these examples:

Form	Part of Speech	Meaning	Example
A. a **couple**	noun	two people who are together	A new **couple** joined our tennis group.
B. a **couple**	noun	some; a few	A **couple** of books are on the table.
C. (to) **couple**	verb	connect, put together	It is possible to **couple** this information with the existing contract.
D. **coupled**	adjective	connected, in addition	The cost of medicine, **coupled** with the lack of physicians, is the root of the healthcare crisis.
E. a **coupling**	noun	a device used to connect two pipes	You're going to need a 3/4-inch **coupling** for this corner.

EXERCISE **8** After studying the information about the word *couple* in the table above, underline *couple* as it appears in the following six sentences. Then write the letter (A, B, C, D, or E) to indicate the usage.

1. _____ Sometimes a word may have a couple of origin possibilities.

2. _____ You have to buy the identical coupling in order to fix the leak.

3. _____ They have been a couple for as long as I can remember.

4. _____ The final exam, coupled with two major reports and lab assignments, makes this one of the most difficult courses at the university.

5. _____ If a couple of important stocks go down, the whole market may go down.

6. _____ After the ceremony, the couple will exit through this door.

THEME: WORD ORIGINS

EXERCISE 9 Underline the correct word in each pair to complete this information about the origins of three food items.

Think about the names of these food items: *strawberry*, *ketchup*, and *asparagus*. Where do you think these names came from? A careful (1) (**analysis / presumption**) of the words within these names can give us a few answers to this question.

Strawberry: Just as it appears to be, the word *strawberry* is actually a combination of the words *straw* and *berry*. Straw here is not the straw you use for drinking but rather is yellowish cut grass. Strawberries grow close to the ground, and farmers used to put straw around the berries to keep the berries off the ground. (2) (**Coupled / Enhanced**) with berry, the word straw indicated the protective (3) (**aid / couple**) so necessary for the successful growth of this fruit. The combination resulted in straw berry, a two-word version. (4) (**Accompanied / Eventually**), it came to be written as a single word—strawberry.

Ketchup: Our English word *ketchup* is from the Chinese word *ke-tsiap*. The Chinese created this great food product in the late seventeenth century. Soon afterward, British explorers came across ketchup in nearby Malaysia and brought it back to the Western world. Fifty years later, this sauce became popular in the American colonies. Around this time, people realized that tomatoes (5) (**accompanied / enhanced**) the flavor of this sauce, so

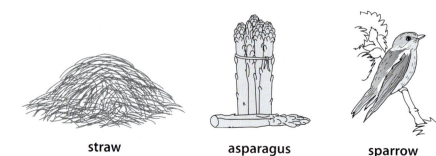

straw   asparagus   sparrow

tomatoes were routinely added to ketchup, and red became the
(6) (**analysis / normal**) color for this sauce. Oddly enough,
ketchup did not contain any tomatoes until the 1790s because
people had the mistaken (7) (**aid / presumption**) that tomatoes
were poisonous! Thus, the English word *ketchup* comes from the
Chinese name for the original sauce, which was neither red nor
tomato-based.

Asparagus: The vegetable name *asparagus* has a bizarre history.
The word *asparagus* means "sparrow grass." What possible connection
could there be between a sparrow, which is the name of a beautiful
little brown bird, and this vegetable? In former times, people were
served asparagus (8) (**accompanied / presumption**) by cooked
sparrows! Because this green, grass-like vegetable was served with
little sparrows, it became known as "sparrow grass," or *asparagus*.

Master Student Tip

A word that ends in *-ed* is usually, but not always, a verb. An *-ed* ending
can also be the past participle of a verb that is being used as an adjective.
Study these examples:

- Regular reading **enhanced** the child's vocabulary dramatically.
  (main verb)

- The computers in the language lab were **enhanced** over spring
  break. They are running much faster than before. (past participle
  used as part of the verb phrase)

- She won the debate with a speech **enhanced** by her superior
  vocabulary. (past participle used as an adjective; a reduced form of
  "that was enhanced")

- The **enhanced** appendix to this edition includes a glossary and
  thesaurus. (past participle used as an adjective)

EXERCISE 10 Write V if the bold vocabulary word is a verb and ADJ if it is an adjective.

1. _____ The new **enhanced** dictionary has information on the origins of many words.

2. _____ The guest speaker at the convention was **accompanied** by his wife and agent as they entered the meeting room.

3. _____ Daily practice **coupled** with periodic review dramatically increases vocabulary retention.

4. _____ Great intelligence has often been **accompanied** by a great sense of humor.

5. _____ After the lecture, the speaker **coupled** the audience into pairs for group work.

6. _____ Proofreading his story before turning it in **enhanced** his prospects for getting it published in the magazine.

Section 3

All the words in Section 3 are of Latin origin. They are grouped together because of their origin and because of the similarity in their verb and noun forms, as you will see in Word List 1.3.

EXERCISE 11 Read Word List 1.3 and its example sentences. Then write a synonym or other information in each box of the third column to help you remember the meaning of the word. Use a dictionary or the information in Exercise 12 to help you with the meaning. The first one has been done for you as an example.

WORD LIST 1.3

Word	Example	Meaning/Notes
compensation	Being fluent in more than one language is the ultimate **compensation** for the serious language learner.	*reward; noun*
discrimination	Speaking the local language can help a minority overcome **discrimination**.	
illustrated	Some learners find it easier to remember words that are **illustrated** instead of just having a simple definition.	
incorporated	This new information will be **incorporated** into the annual report in time for the next meeting.	
integration	The curriculum is designed so that international students experience a smooth **integration** into the regular academic classes.	
isolated	The inability to carry on a conversation using vocabulary appropriate for her age has left her feeling **isolated** and alone.	

13

EXERCISE 12 Match the definitions on the right with the bold vocabulary words on the left. Write the correct letters on the lines.

Nouns

1. _____ compensation

2. _____ discrimination

3. _____ integration

a. Separate treatment based on the differences of a category or group

b. Unifying all the parts together

c. A form of payment given for a service or a loss

Verbs

1. _____ illustrate

2. _____ incorporate

3. _____ isolate

a. Unite with something that already exists

b. Give an example of

c. Separate from others

EXERCISE 13 Complete this chart by writing in the missing word forms. The first row has been done for you as an example.

Verb	Past Tense/Past Participle	Noun
compensate	compensated	compensation
		discrimination
	illustrated	
	incorporated	
		integration
	isolated	

Master Student Tip

When you learn new vocabulary, of course you learn the meanings of the words. However, it is also important to learn the grammar of the new word. One important example is which prepositions you can use after the new words. Remember: When you learn a new word, find out if a certain preposition usually goes with it and then memorize that combination.

EXERCISE 14 Write the correct preposition to complete each sentence: *against, by, for, from, into, of.* The first one has been done for you as an example.

1. Students receive fair compensation _____*for*_____ the hours they spend studying.

2. Have you ever known someone who was discriminated _____ because he or she could not speak English well?

3. His dedication to his studies is illustrated _____ the fact that he is almost always in the library.

4. The instructor has incorporated new multimedia features _____ the curriculum this semester.

5. As the bilingual child's speech develops, eventually there is a peaceful integration _____ the two languages until the child can speak both with equal fluency.

6. If someone is isolated _____ all social interaction starting at a young age, the ability to develop appropriate social interaction is greatly affected.

Section 4

EXERCISE 15 Circle the letter of the correct word that matches each given definition.

1. reduce, make less
    a. enhance
    b. inspect
    c. minimize
    d. reveal

2. provide an example
    a. detect
    b. discriminate
    c. illustrate
    d. integrate

3. improve, make better
    a. enhance
    b. compensate
    c. incorporate
    d. minimize

4. a belief, something we suppose is true
    a. aid
    b. compensation
    c. inspection
    d. presumption

5. but, however
    a attributed
    b. isolated
    c. nevertheless
    d. virtually

6. give the source of
    a. accompany
    b. attribute
    c. enhance
    d. eventual

7. pay someone for work or loss
    a. aid
    b. compensate
    c. inspect
    d. reveal

8. separate from others
    a. attribute
    b. couple
    c. isolate
    d. normal

EXERCISE 16 Fill in each blank with the bold word that best completes the sentence. The first one has been done for you as an example.

1. _Discrimination_____ against people with foreign accents is still an unfortunate and widespread reality. (**Discrimination, Inspection, Integration, Presumption**)

2. A careful _____ of a word's origin can sometimes help you remember the word. (**analysis, detection, elimination, isolation**)

3. A check on the Internet _____ that the vocabulary words used in Section 3 came from Latin. (**aided, attributed, integrated, revealed**)

4. Because of the need for improved dictionaries, almost every publisher _____ produced a new bilingual dictionary with a CD version. (**eventually, nevertheless, normally, virtually**)

5. _____ with information on the spelling and origin of a word, pronunciation notes can be helpful when learning a word. (**Compensated, Coupled, Identical, Incorporated**)

6. A classroom is certainly _____ by the presence of sufficient resources for all students. (**accompanied, enhanced, illustrated, minimized**)

W E B   P O W E R

You will find additional exercises related to the content in this chapter at **http://esl.college.hmco.com/students.**

Architecture and Design Create Atmosphere

FENG SHUI: a way of arranging a room to create the ideal environment in which to live and work

In this chapter, you will

- Become familiar with twenty-four words from the Academic Word List
- Improve your ability to identify relationships using *but* and *so*
- Learn about forming adverbs by using the *-ly* ending
- Practice different word stress patterns

Section 1

EXERCISE **1** Read Word List 2.1. Fill in the boxes in the last column with a predicted meaning for each bold vocabulary word. Then verify your answers by consulting a dictionary. The first one has been done for you as an example.

WORD LIST 2.1

Word	Part of speech	Example	Predicted Meaning
liberal	adjective	Among the cures of Feng Shui, the **liberal** use of metal in main areas of the home helps reduce the negative energy that causes bad luck.	*generous, free*
domestic	adjective	The profound theories and methods of Feng Shui enhance health, prosperity, and **domestic** tranquility.	
underlying	adjective	The **underlying** reason for some health-related problems can be associated with the position of furniture in the home.	
exhibit	verb	For added support, **exhibit** artwork of mountains or tall trees behind your desk.	
radical	adjective	Hanging a mirror across from a window can make a **radical** change in the amount of light in a room.	

Word	Part of speech	Example	Predicted Meaning
resolution	noun	One **resolution** to a cluttered room is to store things in decorative boxes and baskets.	
somewhat	adverb	Living in a small apartment can be **somewhat** challenging	
via	preposition	Many home furnishing companies offer online shopping with product delivery **via** the U.S. Postal Service.	

EXERCISE 2 Match the bold vocabulary word with the appropriate definition. Write the letters on the lines.

1. ———— resolution
2. ———— underlying
3. ———— via
4. ———— radical
5. ———— exhibit
6. ———— domestic
7. ———— somewhat
8. ———— liberal

a. a little
b. free, generous
c. an answer to a problem situation
d. having to do with the home
e. fundamental
f. to show or present
g. by means of
h. drastic

EXERCISE 3 Underline the two choices in each row that can be used in the blank to make logical combinations with the bold vocabulary word. Cross out the word that is not a good combination. The first row has been done for you as an example.

1. a **domestic** ————	fight	animal	~~plastic~~
2. liberal ————	use	wood	view

3. an **underlying** _____   beginning   assumption   principle

4. to **exhibit** _____   problems   dreams   works

5. a **radical** _____   solution   flight   change

6. a **resolution** of _____   a conflict   an argument   a vehicle

7. somewhat _____   complicated   confused   deceased

8. via _____   a brain   the Internet   snail mail

EXERCISE 4 Read these sentences. Connect the second part of each sentence with the first part by writing *but* or *so* to show the relationship between the two parts. (*Note:* Use *but* if the two ideas contrast. Use *so* if the second idea follows logically from the first.) The first one has been done for you as an example.

1. The flight we took to attend the annual meeting of the National Society of Professional Engineers was a **domestic** flight, _____ *but* _____ the flight attendants made the announcements in several languages.

2. It costs $100 to **exhibit** a home design at the design show. I **exhibited** four of my original designs, _____ I was charged $500.

3. The design team leader came up with a **resolution** to all our problems, _____ we were happy.

4. The company sent me the documents **via** e-mail, _____ I didn't have to pay postage.

5. He said he was **somewhat** familiar with the plan for the new bank building, _____ he seemed to know many of the tiniest details about it.

6. The architects' plan for the new hospital was **radical**, _____ everyone, even the conservative members of the planning committee, liked it immediately.

7. At the meeting, I sensed an **underlying** feeling of distrust and disagreement among the members, _____ I felt uncomfortable.

EXERCISE 5   On each line, write a word from the word bank to answer the question correctly. The first one has been done for you as an example.

domestic	liberal	underlying	exhibit
somewhat	radical	resolution	via

1. *exhibit*   Which word can be a noun or a verb?

2. _____ Which word has four different vowels?

3. _____ Which adjective means "new" but is often used in a negative sense?

4. _____ Which word is the opposite of *conservative*?

5. _____ Which word often precedes a method of communication or transportation?

6. _____ Which adjective refers to a house or living area?

7. _____ Which word is often replaced with the idiom "kind of" in conversation?

8. _____ Which adjective describes a feeling that you cannot realize very easily?

9. _____ Which word has a "question word" in it?

10. _____ In your opinion, which word's meaning is the hardest to remember? (Be prepared to explain why.)

Section 2

EXERCISE 6 Read Word List 2.2. Write the part of speech and meaning for each bold vocabulary word as it is used in the corresponding example. Then verify this information with a partner or in a dictionary. The first one has been done for you as an example.

WORD LIST 2.2

Word	Example	Part of Speech & Meaning
dominant	Although various accent colors were used throughout the home, the **dominant** color was blue.	*adjective; main or primary*
scheme	The color **scheme** of the furniture and window treatments focuses on earth tones and natural fibers.	
rational	It is believed that certain colors enhance **rational**, problem-solving thinking.	
dynamic	Red is a **dynamic** color that symbolizes excitement and high energy.	
exposure	For better shade and lower electric bills, designers recommend wooden blinds over drapes for windows with eastern or western **exposure** to the sun.	

Word	Example	Part of Speech & Meaning
flexibility	Reversible bedspreads offer **flexibility** and variety in a child's bedroom.	
finite	Decorator fabrics come in a **finite** set of dimensions.	
theme	Many retailers sell bed linens, draperies, and even furniture all coordinated to popular cartoon **themes**.	

Complete the passage below by writing the appropriate words from Word List 2.2. The first one has been done for you as an example.

Color association is a fascinating subject to explore. The basic
(1) _____*theme*_____ is that colors directly affect
people and their personalities. Some may think that this idea
is not (2) _____, but many believe that
(3) _____ color choices come from a person's
childhood influences. Even though the shades are unlimited, and
therefore are not a (4) _____ set of colors, most
experts classify colors and moods into a dozen or so categories.
For example, green represents nature and relaxation. Because this
soothing color goes with almost any other color, green is believed
to offer great (5) _____ when planning the
décor of a room. In addition, some people believe that
(6) _____ to purple promotes the feeling of
nobility and luxury, a great atmosphere color for a guest room.
On the other hand, a (7) _____ of black with
white, gray, and chrome suggests a contemporary elegance
and sophistication. Finally, if one wants to create a
(8) _____, optimistic effect, it is best to fill
the room with reds and yellows.

Master Student Tip

The vast majority of adjectives are changed to adverbs by simply adding -*ly*; for example, *fresh* becomes *freshly*. If an adjective ends in -*ll*, add only -*y*; for example, *full* becomes *fully*. If an adjective ends in -*ic*, usually add -*ally*; for example, *comic* becomes *comically*.

EXERCISE 7 Change the following vocabulary words to adverbs by adding either -*ly* or -*ally*. Use a dictionary if needed. The first one has been done for you as an example.

Adjective	Adverb
schematic	schematically
domestic	
liberal	
rational	
dynamic	
radical	
thematic	

EXERCISE 8 On each line, write a word from the word bank to answer the question correctly. The first one has been done for you as an example.

dominant	scheme	rational	dynamic
exposure	flexibility	finite	theme

1. Which two words rhyme? _____ scheme, theme _____

2. Which word might you see on a package of film? _____

3. Which word means that the plan was well thought-out?

   _____

4. If you hear that someone is a "**dynamic** speaker," what kind of speaker is that person? _____

5. Which adjective is used to describe the largest group or part?

   _____

6. What is the difference in pronunciation of the letter *y* in the two words that have this letter? _____

7. Do you know the noun *dynamite*? What is the connection in meaning between *dynamite* and **dynamic**? _____

8. Which words means the quantity of something is limited?

   _____

9. Which word means the subject of a written work or of a piece of art?

   _____

10. Which word can have both a positive and negative meaning? When it is positive, it means "an organized plan." When it is negative, it means "a secret plan, usually with a bad purpose"? _____

11. What parts of speech are the words *flex*, *flexible*, and *flexibility*?

    _____

12. Which word can be changed to an antonym by adding the prefix *ir-*?

    _____

Section 3

EXERCISE 9 Read each sentence about architecture. In the second column, write the meaning of the bold vocabulary word. Then write a check mark to indicate if you are sure of this meaning or are guessing from context. Finally, consult a dictionary or ask a classmate to verify your meanings of the words. The first row has been done for you as an example.

Architecture-related sentences	Predicted Meaning	Sure?	Guess?
People who want to build a new home should seek a professional **evaluation** of their home plans before doing anything else.	*an examination*	✔	
Because of the recent rise in the price of lumber, our architect made a slight **adjustment** in the estimated cost of building our house.			
We will not include a swimming pool because it is expensive to operate and because we will not be home enough to enjoy it. **Furthermore**, the initial cost of building a pool is quite high.			
The architect **modified** the plans according to the owner's request for certain changes.			

Architecture-related sentences	Predicted Meaning	Sure?	Guess?
The best architect excels in these pertinent **domains**: technology, business strategy, consulting, and leadership.			
For obvious reasons, the **foundation** of any structure is by far the most important part.			
Sheri Woods graduated with a degree in architectural design in 2003. Although her goal is to work at a large international firm, she is currently employed at a **medium**-sized company.			
A smart architect can draw plans for spaces with all kinds of uses—from formal to **relaxed** and from traditional to modern.			

EXERCISE 10 Read Word List 2.3. Write the part of speech and meaning for each bold vocabulary word as it is used in the corresponding example. Then verify this information with a partner or in a dictionary. The first one has been done for you as an example.

WORD LIST 2.3

Word	Example	Part of Speech & Meaning
adjustment	The electrician made a simple **adjustment** to make the lighting in the kitchen brighter.	*noun; a change*
evaluation	After a careful **evaluation** of restoration costs, the homeowner refinished the hardwood floors instead of covering them with carpet.	
furthermore	Light colors make a room seem larger; **furthermore**, they make it seem brighter, too.	
modified	The architect **modified** the front of the house to include a covered porch.	
domain	The **domain** of architects and designers involves collaboration with several other trades.	
foundation	Recent studies have shown that a properly designed office space is the **foundation** for productivity in the workplace.	
medium	A grouping of several small- and **medium**-sized family photographs adds interest to a room's décor.	
relaxed	Soft, comfortable furniture creates a **relaxed** atmosphere for reading or watching television.	

EXERCISE 11 Write the correct word from Word List 2.3 to complete each sentence. The first one has been done for you as an example.

1. Sometimes just one _____*adjustment*_____ in the way furnishings are organized can make a room seem larger.

2. Problems related to clutter are not only in the _____ of designers but also in that of psychologists.

3. A _____ -sized lamp gives off enough light for reading and without taking up too much room space.

4. Most people think the color blue makes us feel calm and _____.

5. His _____ ideas about how many things he really needs to keep helped him tidy his office.

6. After a careful _____ of the workspace and interviews with employees, an interior designer can offer efficient and professional advice for setting up an office.

7. Most architects think it is important to discuss space planning and colors with clients; _____, it is equally important to address any special needs of workers to create an environment that is beneficial to all.

8. A "good eye" and the ability to draw are the _____ of a successful designer.

Master Student Tip

In learning new words, the sound of a word (or even part of the word) can help you remember that word. Therefore, it is important to learn correct pronunciations. One easy way is to focus on the stress of certain syllables. If a word has more than one syllable, focus on which syllable is stressed (or emphasized). This one technique may help you recall a word better.

EXERCISE 12 Sort the following three-syllable words into the correct stress pattern. Write the words on the lines in the correct columns.

radical   exhibit   foundation   modified
dynamic   rational   finite   domestic
liberal   exposure   adjustment

Stressed First Syllable	Stressed Second Syllable	Stressed Third Syllable
_____	_____	_____
_____	_____	_____
_____	_____	_____
_____	_____	_____
_____	_____	_____
_____	_____	_____

What can you infer about three-syllable words from Exercise 13?

_____

_____

Section 4

EXERCISE 13 Match the appropriate lettered antonym with each bold vocabulary word. Write the letters on the lines.

1. _____ **domestic**

2. _____ **liberal**

3. _____ **modified**

4. _____ **rational**

5. _____ **dynamic**

6. _____ **finite**

7. _____ **somewhat**

8. _____ **radical**

9. _____ **relaxed**

a. unchanged
b. slight
c. a lot
d. without limit
e. tense
f. commercial
g. illogical
h. unenergetic
i. limited

EXERCISE 14 Underline the word in each row that best matches the definition given. The first one has been done for you as an example.

1. to determine the value of
   a. exhibition   **b.** relax   **c.** <u>evaluation</u>   **d.** somewhat

2. having the most control
   a. dominant   **b.** thematic   **c.** liberally   **d.** furthermore

3. a carefully arranged plan
   a. adjustment   **b.** dynamic   **c.** flexible   **d.** scheme

4. the act of making something fit
   a. dominant   **b.** adjustment   **c.** modify   **d.** expose

5. location in reference to sun, wind, etc.
   a. exposure   **b.** finite   **c.** resolve   **d.** via

6. field of activity or influence
   a. infinitely   **b.** irrational   **c.** medium   **d.** domain

7. the ability to bend easily without breaking
   a. domestic   **b.** theme   **c.** flexibility   **d.** underlying

8. in addition
   a. dominant   **b.** modified   **c.** domestic   **d.** furthermore

9. fundamental
   a. evaluate   **b.** adjustment   **c.** underlying   **d.** dynamic

10. the basis on which something rests
    a. liberal   **b.** foundation   **c.** domestic   **d.** relaxed

11. to show or present
    a. exhibit   **b.** furthermore   **c.** rational   **d.** radical

12. a reoccurring subject
    a. flexibility   **b.** finite   **c.** via   **d.** theme

13. by means of
    a. via   **b.** furthermore   **c.** underlying   **d.** liberate

14. of an intermediate degree
    a. exposure   **b.** medium   **c.** schematically   **d.** unmodified

15. having measurable limits
    a. infinite   **b.** finite   **c.** liberally   **d.** somewhat

---

WEB POWER

You will find additional exercises related to the content
in this chapter at **http://esl.college.hmco.com/students.**

The Environment Underwater

In this chapter, you will

- Become familiar with twenty-three words from the Academic Word List
- Explore words with multiple meanings
- Improve your ability to identify as well as form the parts of speech
- Practice distinguishing word stress patterns for nouns and verbs

Section 1

EXERCISE 1 Read Word List 3.1. Fill in the box in the last column with a predicted meaning for each bold vocabulary word. Then verify your answers in a dictionary. The first one has been done for you as an example.

Word	Part of Speech	Example	Predicted meaning
WORD LIST 3.1			
channel	noun	Several commercially targeted species, such as lobsters and cod, rely on the habitat found in a **channel** for survival.	*small river or stream*
ignored	verb	The issue of cruelty to whales is **ignored** by whaling captains.	
mature	adjective	To replenish overfished areas, the government limits clam harvesting to **mature** clams only.	
restore	verb	Certain areas of the Pacific Ocean are protected from fishing boats because this restriction **restores** undersea habitats and life.	
reverse	verb	Laws must be implemented to restrict the passage of vessels in certain areas, which in turn will **reverse** the damage done to deep-sea coral reefs.	
sphere	noun	Underwater explorers can observe an enormous amount of activity through the glass **sphere**-shaped domes of their underwater vehicles.	

Word	Part of Speech	Example	Predicted Meaning
statistics	noun	Recent studies provide useful **statistics** about the chlorophyll concentration in Earth's oceans.	
transport	verb	New submersible vessels can **transport** marine biologists and researchers to two thousand feet below the ocean surface.	

EXERCISE 2 Match the definitions on the right with the bold vocabulary words on the left. Write the correct letters on the lines.

1. _____ sphere

2. _____ transport

3. _____ mature

4. _____ channel

5. _____ restore

6. _____ reverse

7. _____ ignored

8. _____ statistics

a. a narrow stream of water
b. numerical representation of data
c. did not pay attention to
d. to change direction
e. limitations
f. a round shape
g. to bring back to the original state
h. to carry from one place to another
i. advanced in age

EXERCISE 3 Write the appropriate word from Word List 3.1 to complete each sentence. Make sure to check for plural forms, negative forms, and past tense. The first one has been done for you as an example.

1. Under a microscope, the tiny organisms resemble rotating _spheres_____.

2. Unfortunately, the government's plan to correct the species extinction problem _____ the situation.

3. When parts of the natural habitat of the rare oysters began to disappear, the government introduced a great three-point plan which ultimately ———————————— the disappearance.

4. One interesting ———————————— found in the salinity report puzzled the scientists.

5. To ———————————— the ecosystem to a functional state, only ———————————— sea creatures should be fished.

6. The plan to save the mollusks requires that marine biologists ———————————— several species to a well-monitored aquarium for breeding.

7. The spawning salmon were ———————————— to an area of the river that allowed researchers to observe their behavior.

8. The fishing boats ———————————— not only the No Trespassing sign but also the Coast Guard's signals to leave the area.

EXERCISE 4   In the following sentences, the verbs are being used with additional meanings. Guess the meaning of each bold vocabulary word as it is used in the sentence. Then write the predicted meaning after the word.

channel (*v.*) —————————————————————————————————
   Information regarding illegal fishing practices should be **channeled** to the proper authorities.

channel (*n.*) —————————————————————————————————
   New **channels** of exploration are investigating the ecological effect of water contamination.

mature (*v.*) —————————————————————————————————
   Coral reefs **mature** at a very slow rate and take years to establish.

Section 2

EXERCISE 5 Read Word List 3.2. Write the part of speech and meaning for each bold vocabulary word as it is used in the corresponding example. Then verify this information with a partner or in a dictionary. The first one has been done for you as an example.

WORD LIST 3.2		
Word	**Example**	**Part of Speech & Meaning**
acknowledged	The government **acknowledged** the threat to undersea life by passing the Ocean Habitat Protection Act of 2003.	*verb; to recognize*
evolution	Government regulatory agencies are concerned with the future **evolution** of marine ecology.	
exceed	The number of unexplored coastal areas in the world **exceeds** the number of researchers available to study them.	
imposed	Ocean zoning has been **imposed** on various regions as a way to manage marine ecosystems.	
phenomenon	Ocean observatories study the **phenomenon** of volcanic activity and climate changes.	
project	High school students in Hawaii participated in a **project** investigating whale songs.	
rigid	Because deep-sea coral is not **rigid** or strong, it is easily crushed by passing bottom trawlers.	
successive	Oceanographers have studied the ocean for centuries by using ships, but **successive** steps are being taken to develop less limiting means of collecting information.	

EXERCISE 6 Complete the passage below by writing the appropriate words from Word List 3.2. The first one has been done for you as an example.

The Galapagos Islands are fascinating for several reasons. In the 1800s, historian Charles Darwin traveled there to observe examples of fauna and flora. What was at first thought of as a (1) _phenomenon_____ was later explained by Charles Darwin as he made observations during the nineteen-year (2) _____. Because of the limited species and isolation, Darwin often described the island as a "living laboratory of (3) _____" to refer to the changes that had taken place there over the course of history.

Another reason why the Galapagos Islands are fascinating is that the underwater volcanic activity (4) _____ any other on Earth. In fact, (5) _____ volcanic eruptions gently emit lava, which cools and becomes (6) _____. The amazing underwater formations that result are abundant in marine life.

Master Student Tip

   Words have many forms, and it is important for you to learn more than just one form of a word. Three of the most important forms of any word are noun, verb, and adjective. Focus on the endings (or suffixes) that create these three forms of a word.

EXERCISE 7 Change the following word forms from Sections 1 and 2 into nouns. Pay careful attention to spelling changes. Use a dictionary to check the spellings. The first one has been done for you as an example.

1. **mature**   _maturation_____

2. **impose**   _____

3. **restore**   _____

4. **transport** _____

5. **project**   _____

6. **rigid**   _____

EXERCISE 8 On each line, write a word from the word bank to answer the question correctly. The first one has been done for you as an example.

ignore	sphere	acknowledgment	reverse
phenomenon	impose	project	evolutionist

1. How many verbs appear in the list? _four_

2. Which word can be used as both a noun and a verb by changing only the syllable stress? _____

3. Which word does not have a noun form? _____

4. Which word means "one who studies the process of animal or plant development"? _____

5. Which word means "to go in the opposite direction?"

   _____

6. Which words have a special spelling for the /f/ sound?

   _____

7. Which words have four syllables? _____

Section 3

EXERCISE 9 Read Word List 3.3. Write the part of speech and meaning for each bold vocabulary word as it is used in the example sentence. Then verify this information with a partner or in a dictionary. The first one has been done for you as an example.

WORD LIST 3.3		
Word	**Example**	**Part of speech & meaning**
abandon	Even if placing themselves in danger, mother whales will not **abandon** their young.	*verb; to leave*
adaptation	The **adaptation** of sea life to underwater pipelines has caused permanent changes in the ecosystem.	
constitutional	The **constitutional** aspects of environmental protection have led to legislation that effectively preserves sea life.	
constraints	Fishing **constraints** can eliminate considerable damage to delicate marine habitats.	
disposal	Many nations prohibit the **disposal** of toxic waste into rivers, lakes, and oceans.	
insert	**Inserted** in the amazing coral reefs of John Pennekamp State Park is the famous statue *Christ of the Abyss*.	
voluntary	**Voluntary** consumption of low-grade sea urchin products, as opposed to those of higher quality, has led to a blossoming sea urchin market in Australia.	

EXERCISE 10 Identify the following word pairs as either synonyms or antonyms. The first one has been done for you as an example.

1. **adaptation**, modification   *synonym* _____

2. **constitutional**, nonessential   _____

3. **voluntary**, unwilling   _____

4. **insert**, remove   _____

5. **constraints**, limitations   _____

6. **disposal**, elimination   _____

7. **abandon**, retain   _____

Master Student Tip

Many English words can be both nouns and verbs. Both forms usually have the same pronunciation. However, some of these words are pronounced differently. Often the noun forms carry stress on the first syllable, but the verb forms carry stress on the second syllable.

An example is the word *present*. When pronounced as a noun, the stress is on the first syllable: *PRES·ent*. When pronounced as a verb, the stress is on the second syllable: *pre·SENT*.

Because the sound of a word helps us remember words, pay attention to the stress of the syllables in your new vocabulary.

EXERCISE 11 Practice pronouncing these bold vocabulary words. Then practice pronouncing them in the sentences. Listen for syllable stress. Underline the stressed syllables in each word pair. The first one has been done for you as an example.

project

The **pro·ject** of protecting certain undersea species is an enormous task.

Marine biologists **proj·ect** undersea explorations well in advance.

insert

The document **insert** describes the rules and regulations for diving in the marine preserve.

Researchers will **insert** an underwater camera near the seawall to monitor passing vessels.

transport

The primary form of **transport** for vehicles is the waterways along the coast.

Ferries **transport** scuba-diving enthusiasts to the coral reef twice a day.

EXERCISE 12 In each row, write the best choice to complete each phrase. The first one has been done for you as an example.

1. constraining _situation_   situation   geographical

2. involuntary _____   actions   ocean

3. disposal _____   of   out

4. _____ abandonment   walked on   accused of

5. adapted _____   from   against

6. constitutes _____   an agreement   advanced

7. a very _____ insert   respect   informative

Section 4

EXERCISE 13 Write answers from the word bank to complete the sentences. The first one has been done for you as an example.

Fascinating Facts about the Ocean

evolution	sphere	voluntarily	statistics
exceed	adaptation	reverse	insert
transport	rigid	mature	constitutional

1. More than three billion years ago, life began its _evolution_ in the seas.

2. The _____ of coral for bone grafts in humans is possible because of coral's similarity to the architecture and chemistry of human bone.

3. The _____ of the bluefin tuna reveal that it is not only the fastest marine fish, able to swim up to fifty-five miles per hour, but also the largest, reaching up to 1,500 pounds.

4. The speed at which penguins "fly" underwater can _____ twenty-five miles per hour.

5. Algae with _____ shells, called diatoms, are used to make pet litter, pool filters, cosmetics, and toothpaste.

6. Because the blood vessels of the blue whale are so large, it is possible to _____ a full-grown trout into them.

7. Mussels and tubeworms _____ gather around fractures in the sea floor because of the sulfur compounds the fractures release.

8. The heart of a _____ blue whale is about the size of a small car.

9. The _____ structure of hydrothermal vents, cracks in the sea floor, is unique because it is the only known ecosystem that functions on chemicals instead of on solar energy.

10. Often, green turtles will _____ their eggs as many as 1,400 miles before laying them in a nest to hatch.

EXERCISE 14 For each row, write the best answer to complete the phrase or sentence. The first one has been done for you as an example.

1. a spherically-shaped		
vessel	researcher	vessel
2. the restoration of		
_____	a coral reef	a study
3. channeled		
_____	down the river	over the river
4. They **abandon** their unhealthy		
_____.	babies	inspection
5. It transports		
_____.	visitors	acknowledgment
6. They implemented **successive**		
_____.	habits	measures
7. We were **acknowledged**		
_____.	by the discovery	for the discovery
8. They sought to **reverse**		
_____.	the **channel**	the process
9. phenomenal		
_____	statistics	normal
10. the **disposal**		
_____	in the fish	of the fish
11. The new rules were **imposed**		
_____.	on fishermen	in fishermen
12. unconstrained		
_____	fishing practices	**successive**
13. the projection of		
_____	exceedingly	population
14. ignorance of the		
_____	consequences	radical

EXERCISE 15   In each row, circle the word that is a synonym for the underlined word.

1. a fundamental right

    minimal   constitutional   complex

2. limiting regulations

    generous   domestic   constraining

3. a(n) inconvenience

    imposition   oversight   evidence

4. a(n) estimation of costs

    balance   limit   projection

5. a(n) changing sea life

    evolving   basic   previous

6. recognition for scientific discoveries

    exhibition   acknowledgment   flexibility

7. neglect ecological concerns

    ignore   resolve   reverse

8. a thriving, protected waterway

    disposal   channel   project

9. reach a full-grown state

    voluntary   phenomenal   mature

10. hard, protective shell

    rigid   soft   flexible

WEB POWER

You will find additional exercises related to the content in this chapter at **http://esl.college.hmco.com/students.**

Education: The Art and Science of Teaching Others

In this chapter, you will

- Become familiar with twenty-four words from the Academic Word List
- Learn about the use of prepositions after certain vocabulary words
- Examine the keyword method, a technique to help you remember words
- Study word form changes

Section 1

EXERCISE 1 Read Word List 4.1. Then write a synonym or other piece of information about the bold vocabulary word to help you remember the meaning of the word. Use a dictionary or the information in Exercise 2 to help you. The first one is done for you as an example.

WORD LIST 4.1

Word	Part of Speech	Example	Meaning/Notes
administration	noun	The **administration** has decided to update the entire curriculum at the end of this semester.	*organizers or leaders*
cooperation	noun	With a little **cooperation**, a group project can be more fun and productive than an individual project.	
diversity	noun	The mixture of cultures in the United States creates great **diversity** in classrooms these days.	
formula	noun	Our instructor suggested an excellent **formula** for remembering difficult vocabulary words. It really works!	
monitoring	noun	After **monitoring** her students' progress, the instructor determined that they needed more review before the final exam.	
policy	noun	The school **policy** states that students must maintain at least a C average to graduate.	

Word	Part of Speech	Example	Meaning/Notes
priority	noun	Raising standards in all schools is the top **priority** for education in our district.	
regulations	noun	The state government pays each local school a set amount of money based on **regulations** made under the so-called Schools for All law passed last year.	
strategies	noun	A successful student uses many **strategies** to learn and remember new vocabulary.	
theory	noun	Do you have a **theory** to explain why some students are clearly more successful than others?	

EXERCISE 2 In each row, circle the answer choice that is related to the bold vocabulary word.

1. **administration**	followers	leaders
2. **cooperation**	do it separately	do it together
3. **diversity**	a big group	a mixed group
4. **formula**	a recipe	a receipt
5. **monitoring**	preserving	observing
6. **policy**	a rule	a choice
7. **priority**	most difficult	most important
8. **regulation**s	guidelines	remarks
9. **strategies**	techniques	effects
10. **theory**	fact	idea

EXERCISE 3 In each sentence, underline the bold vocabulary word that is covered in Section 1. Then circle the letter that logically completes the sentence.

1. During the graduation, the head of the **administration**
   a. gave a speech and handed out the diplomas.
   b. listened to a speech and received a diploma.

2. The instructor guessed that the students displayed no **cooperation** on the project because it was
   a. organized and attractive.
   b. disorganized and unattractive.

3. The **diversity** in urban classrooms is always much more than in rural classrooms because, in big cities, students
   a. come from many different countries.
   b. all live in the same country now.

4. The best **formula** for learning and remembering new vocabulary words is
   a. reading quickly and then taking a nap.
   b. reading carefully and then taking notes.

5. By **monitoring** students' facial expressions, an instructor should be able to determine
   a. if the students understand what is being discussed.
   b. if the students are intelligent and wealthy.

6. If the school **administration** implements a new **policy**, then probably
   a. things will change.
   b. things will stay the same.

7. Because education is such a **priority** to the taxpayers, the governor has decided to give more tax money to
   a. build more roads.
   b. build more schools.

8. The college **regulations** state that to be hired for the teaching position, the applicant must have a master's degree. Harold does not have his master's degree yet, so he
   a. should apply for the job.
   b. should not apply for the job.

9. Of all the **strategies** she has tried for developing rich vocabulary, Marjorie has found the keyword method to be the most effective. Thus, she has finally
   a. found an effective method of learning.
   b. realized that she is a very effective learner.

10. Hassan says that watching television really helped him **develop** a rich vocabulary. Hassan's instructor, however, does not support this theory for advanced language learning. Hassan's instructor
    a. thinks that television will not help advanced learners.
    b. knows that television will not help advanced learners.

Master Student Tip

When you learn new vocabulary, you must, of course, learn the meanings of the words. However, it is also important to learn the grammar of the words. Many words can have more than one part of speech. Remember: When you learn a new word, find out if it has multiple forms. This way, you can earn two or three words for the price of one.

EXERCISE 4 Complete this chart with the missing word forms. The first row has been done for you as an example.

Verb	Noun	Adjective	Adverb
administer	administration	administrative	administratively
			cooperatively
		diverse	
prioritize			
	regulation		
		strategic	

Section 2

EXERCISE **5** Read Word List 4.2. Then in the last box in each row, write a synonym or other information about the bold vocabulary word to help you remember the meaning. Use a dictionary or the information in Exercise 6 to help you with the meanings.

WORD LIST 4.2

Word	Part of Speech	Example	Meaning/Notes
access	noun	Students who did not have **access** to dictionaries during the assignment did not perform as well as those who used dictionaries.	*ability to use*
comprehension	adjective	The **comprehension** questions at the end of the article check if students understand what they have read.	
crucial	adjective	If you do not understand a word, it is **crucial** that you look it up in a dictionary.	
definite	adjective	Methods such as problem-based learning claim to offer **definite** advantages in the classroom.	
excluded	adjective	A good instructor will involve the entire class so that no one feels **excluded**.	

Word	Part of Speech	Example	Meaning/Notes
ministry	noun	After graduation, some students may want to apply for a government job at the **Ministry** of Education.	
publication	noun	Because of excessive grammatical errors, the article was not considered for **publication** in the magazine.	
summary	noun	Your **summary** of the article should be much shorter than the article itself.	

EXERCISE 6 In each row, circle the answer choice that is related to the bold vocabulary word.

1. access	enter	exit
2. comprehension	misunderstand	understand
3. crucial	dangerous	essential
4. definite	changing	unchanging
5. excluded	left out	left over
6. ministry	helpful organization	helpful idea
7. publication	something to read	something to watch
8. summary	longer version	shorter version

EXERCISE 7 Study the information about the word *access* in the table. In each sentence that follows, underline the form of *access* used. Then, on the line, write the letter (A, B, C, D) to indicate the usage.

ACCESS

The word *access* has several forms with different meanings, but all the meanings are related to "reaching" or "entering." Consider these examples:

Form	Part of Speech	Meaning	Example
A. (to) access	verb	to get into; to enter	She **accessed** her account with her ATM card.
B. access	noun	ability or permission to use	Students have **access** to study materials in the library.
C. access	noun	a way or means of reaching or entering a place	The only **access** to the cafeteria was through the gym.
D. access	adjective	related to entering	I was locked out of the building because I forgot the **access** code.

1. _____ Everyone has access to the student support center.

2. _____ All access roads to the stadium were closed off during the homecoming game.

3. _____ Please leave me the extra key so that I can access the game room while you are out of town.

4. _____ If you have access to the Internet, I suggest that you use it.

5. _____ After rocks blocked the path, we were forced to find another access to the mountain peak.

6. _____ Students can only access the school's database through computers on campus.

Master Student Tip

The task of learning and remembering new vocabulary words can be daunting. However, one technique that works for many students is the "keyword method." In this technique, learners first select a word in their native language that looks or sounds like the target English word. Then they form a mental association or picture between the English word and the native-language word. For example, an English speaker learning the Malay word for door, *pintu*, might associate this target word with the English words *pin* and *into*. The learner would then visualize someone putting a "pin into a door" to open it. This could help the learner remember *pintu* for door.

EXERCISE **8** Create a mental association for each bold vocabulary word in this chart. Sharing them with the rest of your class can help you develop better mental images, too.

New Vocabulary	Your Memory Key
access	
comprehension	
crucial	
definite	
excluded	
ministry	
publication	
summary	

Section 3

EXERCISE 9 Read Word List 4.3. Then in the last box in each row, write a synonym or other piece of information about the bold vocabulary word to help you remember the meaning. The first one has been done for you as an example.

Word	Part of Speech	Example	Meaning/Notes
WORD LIST 4.3			
bias	noun	The difference in personality suggests that every student will have a **bias** toward one learning style or another.	*preference*
conference	noun	The newest theories on second-language acquisition were explained at the teachers' **conference**.	
dramatic	adjective	A **dramatic** increase in class participation occurred immediately before the final exam.	
generated	verb	The brainstorming activity **generated** many useful ideas.	
solely	adverb	The administration tries to base its policies **solely** on the best interest of the students.	
thesis	noun	As a final project, students are to research a topic of interest and then write a **thesis**.	

EXERCISE 10 Use vocabulary words from Word List 4.3 to fill in the blanks in this passage about Howard Gardner's **theory** of multiple intelligences. The first one has been done for you as an example.

The **theory** of multiple intelligences suggests a number of distinct forms of intelligence that each individual possesses in varying degrees. Respected author and Harvard University professor Howard Gardner, Ph.D., identified seven different types of intelligence. In 1984, at an international (1) _conference_ of educators, he proposed the (2) _____ **theory** that a person can demonstrate different levels of intelligence for each of the seven types. Gardner further suggested that because of each person's natural ability in any one of these seven intelligences, each person would naturally possess a preference for, or (3) _____ toward, the style of learning that most closely corresponded to her or his strengths. The seven intelligences that Gardner identified were linguistic, logical-mathematical, musical, spatial, bodily-kinesthetic, interpersonal, and intrapersonal. Gardner's new **theory** (4) _____ much controversy among teachers who had for years relied (5) _____ on the old-fashioned (and frequently boring) lecture style of teaching—talking the whole time while students just listened and quickly took notes. In the years that followed, Gardner developed his controversial (6) _____ in books in which he wrote, "It is very important that a teacher take individual differences among kids very seriously. The bottom line is a deep interest in children and how their minds are different from one another, and in helping them use their minds well."

EXERCISE 11 Match the definitions on the right with the keywords on the left.

1. _____ bias

2. _____ conference

3. _____ thesis

4. _____ sole

5. _____ generate

6. _____ dramatic

a. a meeting for consultation or discussion

b. to produce, cause to exist

c. a report that presents an original point of view from research

d. entire, exclusive

e. a preference that inhibits fair judgment

f. showing strong action or emotion

EXERCISE 12 In each blank, write the correct preposition: *against, by, for, from, into, of.* The first one has been done for you as an example.

1. Students receive fair compensation _for_____ the hours they spend studying.

2. Some people discriminate _____ persons who do not speak English well.

3. Her dedication to her studies is illustrated _____ the fact that she is almost always in the library.

4. The instructor has incorporated many new multimedia features _____ the curriculum this semester.

5. As the bilingual child's speech develops, eventually a peaceful integration _____ the two languages occurs until the child can speak both with equal fluency.

6. If someone is isolated _____ all social interaction starting at a young age, her or his ability to develop appropriate social interaction is greatly affected.

EXERCISE 13 Write an answer to these questions about the words in the word bank. The first one has been done for you as an example.

bias	conference	dramatic	generated	solely	thesis

1. Which two words have only the two vowels *e* and *o*? <u>solely</u>

2. Which word means "a meeting"? _____

3. Which word can be a past participle? _____

4. Which word is an adverb? _____

5. Which words can be nouns? _____

6. Which word is only an adjective? _____

7. Which word is a type of **publication**? _____

8. Which word can be used before the words movie, story, and ending? _____

Section 4

EXERCISE 14 Write the part(s) of speech next to each bold vocabulary word from this chapter. The first one has been done for you as an example.

1. access   *noun, verb*

2. administration   _____

3. bias   _____

4. comprehension   _____

5. conference   _____

6. cooperation   _____

7. crucial   _____

8. definite   _____

9. diversity   _____

10. dramatic   _____

11. excluded   _____

12. formula   _____

13. generated   _____

14. ministry   _____

15. monitoring   _____

16. policy   _____

17. priority   _____

18. publication   _____

19. regulations   _____

20. solely   _____

21. strategies   _____

22. summary   _____

23. theory   _____

24. thesis   _____

EXERCISE 15 Write words from the three word lists in this chapter to fill in the blanks in this reading about Robert Gagné's nine steps for organizing lesson plans to create ideal conditions for learning. The first one has been done for you as an example.

The instructional (1) _theory_ most frequently associated with Robert Gagné involves creating an environment or condition in which learning can most naturally occur. Many of the best teaching (2) _____ currently used in our classrooms today are actually based on Gagné's nine steps. In this theory, the first of Gagné's nine educational steps is to gain attention of the learner. For this reason, presenting the lesson in a (3)_____ or interesting way is a top (4) _____. The second step in the process is to present the learner with the lesson's objective by identifying a (5) _____ or specific problem. The third step is for the instructor to help the learner (6) _____ information relevant to the topic that is already familiar to the learner. The fourth step is to isolate the objective again by clearly defining it. In step five, the learner builds confidence and familiarity through comprehensible, real-world examples of the target concept. Step six requires some (7) _____ on the part of the students. Test their (8) _____ by putting them in problem-solving groups and determine if the correct results are (9) _____. After closely (10) _____ the responses, the instructor goes to step seven, which involves providing constructive feedback on the learners' performances. Further assessing learner progress, as defined by step eight, can be done by assigning grades or requesting a teacher-student (11) _____. The ninth and final step in Gagné's **theory** is to enhance retention by recycling the objective over time through additional practice opportunities. In (12) _____, Robert Gagné's **theory** suggests that the conditions in which a lesson is presented are as (13) _____ to the learning process as the lesson itself.

WEB POWER

You will find additional exercises related to the content in this chapter at **http://esl.college.hmco.com/students**.

Issues in the Healthcare Industry

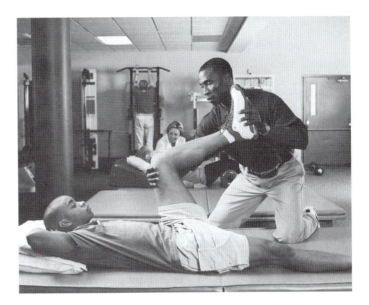

In this chapter, you will

- Become familiar with twenty-three words from the Academic Word List
- Improve your ability to identify parts of speech
- Learn about the importance of word collocations
- Practice new word forms by adding suffixes

Section 1

EXERCISE **1** Study Word List 5.1. Write the part of speech and meaning for each bold vocabulary word as it is used in the example sentence. Then verify this information with a partner or in a dictionary. The first one has been done for you as an example.

WORD LIST 5.1

Word	Example	Part of Speech & Meaning
registered	A **registered** nurse is trained in reading medical charts and administering medications on behalf of the physician.	adjective; one who has been recognized by an association
enforcement	Officers in law **enforcement** can offer basic first aid if needed at the scene of automobile accidents.	
interval	It is recommended that patients refrain from taking large doses of pain-reducing medications over long **intervals** of time.	
deny	Some insurance policies **deny** coverage for medical expenses that are not first approved by the primary care physician.	
submitted	The patient **submitted** her insurance claims by the deadline.	
transmission	The **transmission** of diseases is an issue that both society and government must address.	
practitioner	A nurse **practitioner** assists physicians in the pre-evaluation of patients.	

EXERCISE 2 Complete the passage below by writing the appropriate words from Word List 5.1. The first one has been done for you as an example.

Vaccinations are a part of everyone's life at one time or another. Shortly after birth, infants receive their first vaccinations. Once they reach school age, a series of vaccinations is required in order to prevent the (1) _transmission_ of diseases such as measles, mumps, and rubella. A nurse (2) _____ or (3) _____ nurse will explain to the parents at what (4) _____ each required shot will be administer. Travelers are also often faced with vaccination requirements. Some countries will (5) _____ a visitor a visa if the proper vaccination forms have not been completed and (6) _____. The (7) _____ of these vaccinations ensures the health of the general public and reduces the likelihood of disease epidemics.

EXERCISE 3 The words in Word List 5.1 are often found in various forms. Complete each sentence below by writing the appropriate form of the given bold vocabulary word. Make changes for parts of speech as needed.

practice

A _practicing_ physician is a doctor who sees patients on a regular basis.

Dr. Wilson's medical _____ has been located in the downtown area for the past twenty years.

transmit

The initialism STD stands for "sexually _____ disease."

Most germs are easily _____ through saliva and mucus.

register

The hospital receptionist consulted the admission _____ to find out which room was assigned to the patient.

From the analysis, lab professionals noted that high levels of mercury _____ in the blood samples.

Section 2

EXERCISE 4 Study Word List 5.2. Fill in the boxes in the last column with a predicted meaning for each bold vocabulary word. Then verify your answers by checking in a dictionary. The first one has been done for you as an example.

WORD LIST 5.2

Word	Part of speech	Example	Predicted Meaning
tension	noun	A common cause of migraines is stress and muscular **tension** in the shoulders and neck.	*not in a relaxed state*
revision	noun	The most recent **revision** of this state's vaccination policies included a mandatory chicken pox vaccine for all children entering kindergarten.	
external	adjective	**External** symptoms can often signal internal health conditions.	
maximum	adjective	A **maximum** out-of-pocket expense limit is usually reached early during a fiscal year.	
cited	adjective	The latest data **cited** at the medical conference supported the government's theory of a growing epidemic of the disease.	
recovery	adjective	The **recovery** time for a stroke patient can range from months to years, depending on the severity of the stroke.	

Word	Part of speech	Example	Predicted Meaning
contrary	adjective	**Contrary** to previous years, many terminally-ill patients are now seeking home healthcare as a medical option.	
release	verb	Patients are not **released** from quarantine units until they are no longer infectious to others.	

EXERCISE 5   Write the word from Word List 5.2 that is most opposite in meaning to the words below. The first one has been done for you as an example.

1. minimum   *maximum*

2. withhold   _____

3. inside   _____

4. laxness   _____

5. original   _____

6. similar   _____

7. not quoted   _____

8. worsening   _____

EXERCISE **6** The words in Word List 5.2 are often found in various forms. Complete each sentence by writing the appropriate bold vocabulary word given. Make changes for parts of speech as needed. The first one has been done for you as an example.

cited

The bibliographical _citation_ tells the reader in which medical journal the study is found.

tension

Critical-care wards are _____ environments because of the seriousness of the patient's medical state.

As sensation returned to his legs, the man was soon able to _____ up his muscles.

contrary

Because the diagnosis of the primary physician was _____ to that of the specialist, a third physician was called in to examine the patient.

Results of the two studies provided _____ evidence on whether the natural remedies can actually cure the common cold.

recovery

She can _____ completely with the help of an occupational therapist.

Patients _____ from cancer try to maintain a positive attitude as part of the healing process.

Master Student Tip

▼ When you learn a new word, try to memorize a small natural phrase. This naturally occurring phrase is called a collocation. For example, you just learned the noun *recovery*, which is from the verb *recover*. If you are not sure of the meaning of *recover*, learn the collocation "*recover* from an illness." Knowing that *recover* means "to get well" is good, but is just passive knowledge of the word. However, being able to use the word in a sentence is active knowledge, and knowing the collocations of a word can help you use words actively.

EXERCISE 7 This exercise lets you experience the difference between "active" vocabulary and "passive" vocabulary. Read the following words in isolation, and then try to predict their meanings.

1. auspicious _____

2. putrid _____

3. array _____

Now read those same words in context, and then try to predict the meanings of the words.

1. The well-dressed guests, extravagant meal, and elegant atmosphere clearly showed it was an auspicious occasion. _____

_____

2. Days after the garbage workers went on strike, trash began piling up on the streets, and the putrid odor was becoming quite unbearable.

_____

3. All the guests were happy with the wide array of fun activities available at the resort. _____

The key collocations here are:

1. auspicious + occasion

2. putrid + odor

3. wide + array + of + activities (OR: choices, options)

Section 3

EXERCISE 8 Study Word List 5.3. Fill in the boxes in the last column with a predicted meaning for each bold vocabulary word. Then verify your answers by checking in a dictionary. The first one has been done for you as an example.

WORD LIST 5.3

Word	Part of speech	Example	Predicted Meaning
duration	noun	The **duration** of the therapy is usually based on how the patient's body responds to the medication.	*the length of time something lasts*
uniform	noun	Most healthcare professionals who work in hospitals wear **uniforms**.	
capacity	noun	During times of national disasters, medical facilities exceed **capacity** and must set up temporary centers to treat all the patients.	
interpretation	noun	To make a diagnosis, physicians rely heavily on the **interpretation** of medical test results and patient history.	
consultation	noun	Before undergoing major surgery, most patients prefer a **consultation** with a second physician.	
assigned	verb	Occupational therapists are **assigned** to individuals who have lost their ability to function in the workplace.	

Word	Part of speech	Example	Predicted Meaning
equipment	noun	Home healthcare agencies provide a variety of services and **equipment** for the ill.	
ideology	noun	The Hippocratic oath is based on the **ideology** that physicians will prescribe treatments only for healing purposes.	

EXERCISE 9 Match each phrase below with a bold vocabulary word from Word List 5.3. The first one has been done for you as an example.

1. Tools and machines   _equipment_

2. Another opinion   _____

3. Amount of time   _____

4. Beliefs or values   _____

5. Instructed to attend to   _____

6. Amount of load   _____

7. All the same   _____

8. One's understanding   _____

EXERCISE 10 Categorize the following words and phrases into groups. Write each one in the appropriate shape below. One has been done for you as an example.

assigned to   **capacity**   **equipment**   how long something
consult with   **duration**   machines   lasts
given to   **ideology**   length of time   hear another person's
instruments   **interpret**   similar garments   view
beliefs   philosophy   get someone's opinion   understand the
uniform   concepts   **maximum** amount   meaning of

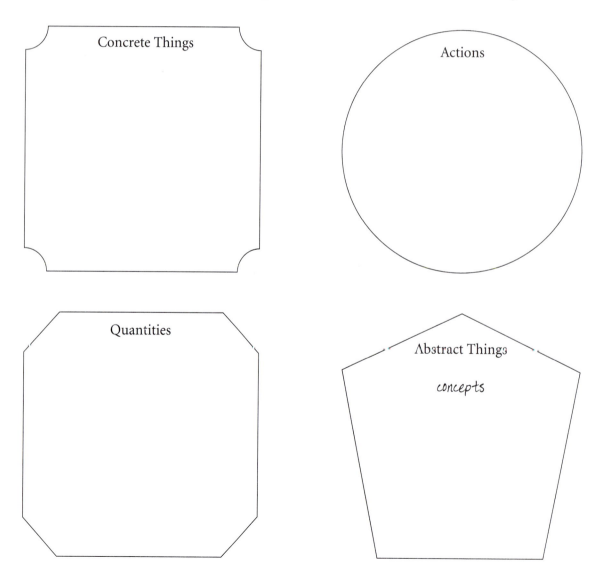

Concrete Things

Actions

Quantities

Abstract Things

concepts

> **Master Student Tip**
>
> Using prefixes and suffixes is one of the easiest ways to increase your vocabulary. Knowing more than one form of a word is important to increasing your vocabulary. Some of the most productive suffixes for making noun forms are -*tion*, -*sion*, and -*ment*. Therefore, the verb form can easily be determined by removing these noun suffixes and adjusting for spelling. Whenever you learn a word ending in -*tion*, -*sion*, or -*ment*, stop to imagine the word without this noun ending. The result could be a brand new verb for you!

EXERCISE 11 On the line below each noun, write the verb form. The first one has been done for you as an example.

misinterpretation   enforcement   tension   regulation

misinterpret   _____   _____   _____

reassignment   elimination   equipment   cooperation

_____   _____   _____   _____

EXERCISE 12 Write the appropriate verb form from Exercise 11 in the blanks to complete the sentences. The first one has been done for you as an example.

1. The nurse was _reassigned_____ to the Intensive Care Ward because of lack of personnel there.

2. Insurance companies strictly _____ their "Pre-existing Conditions" requirement.

3. Complex medical terminology can cause a patient to _____ important medical information.

4. Physical therapy treatments can often _____ the need for surgery.

5. During a spasm, the muscles _____ up and tremble.

6. Pain medication is often administered and _____ by the patient through a hand-held pump-type device.

7. Most walk-in clinics are sufficiently _____ to handle non-life-threatening situations.

8. The successful treatment of any emergency room patient requires the various medical professionals who work there everyday to _____.

Section 4

EXERCISE 18 Add a prefix or suffix from the box to the keyword in each phrase to form a new word. Write the new word on the line. The first one is done for you as an example.

re-   mis-   in-   -ate   -er   -sion   un-   -able   de-

1. To interpret incorrectly   _misinterpret_

2. One who practices   _____

3. not capable   _____

4. Something transmitted   _____

5. To assign to a different task   _____

6. Is not deniable   _____

7. The process of reversing registration _____

8. To interpret again   _____

EXERCISE 14   Circle the correct word choice that is a synonym for the word or phrase. The first one has been done for you as an example.

1. Opposite
   a. contrary
   b. release
   c. revised
   d. uniformity

2. The time between events
   a. enforce
   b. interval
   c. max
   d. reinterpretation

3. The act of making sure rules are followed
   a. enforcement
   b. deregistration
   c. practitioners
   d. externalize

4. The amount of time something lasts
   a. cites
   b. duration
   c. reassigned
   d. ideology

5. Understanding in a different way
   a. reassigning
   b. recovering
   c. reinterpreting
   d. releasing

6. The act of lowering oneself
   a. duration
   b. submission
   c. tension
   d. transmission

7. Evenness; consistency
   a. capacity
   b. contrarily
   c. ideology
   d. uniformity

8. The degree of tightness
   a. revision
   b. submission
   c. tension
   d. transmission

EXERCISE 15 Complete the grid with the correct word forms. Use a dictionary if needed. The completed grid will include most of the vocabulary words from this chapter. The first row has been completed for you as an example.

Noun	Adjective	Verb	Adverb
interpretation	interpretative	interpret	
		maximize	
registration			
		consult	
	external		
assignment			
		cite	
	recoverable		
denial			
			ideologically
		transmit	
revision			
			tensely
uniformity			

```
WEB POWER
You will find additional exercises related to the content in
this chapter at http://esl.college.hmco.com/students.
```

The Business Evolution

In this chapter, you will

- Become familiar with twenty-three words from the Academic Word List
- Read about similar but different word pairs
- Practice the spelling patterns of words ending with *-y*
- Compare common usages for certain words

Section 1

EXERCISE 1 Study Word List 6.1. Fill in the boxes in the last column with a predicted meaning for each bold vocabulary word. Then verify your predictions by checking in a dictionary. The first one has been done for you as an example.

WORD LIST 6.1			
Word	Part of speech	Example	Predicted Meaning
arbitrary	adjective	The increase in global advertising sales is not a result of **arbitrary** occurrences, but rather the rise in Internet users worldwide.	*occurring without a specific pattern or reason.*
converted	verb	The accounting department **converted** all the records to a faster, more user-friendly software.	
device	noun	That professional uses an electronic **device** to keep track of appointments.	
emerged	verb	Wireless ads have **emerged** as the leading form of advertising among marketing specialists.	
guarantee	noun	The "limited **guarantee**" found with many products covers replacement costs for the first ninety days after the purchase.	

Word	Part of speech	Example	Predicted Meaning
mode	noun	SMS (short messaging service) offers users an efficient **mode** of communication.	
implicit	adjective	Although not directly stated, the advertisement's **implicit** message was that the product was completely waterproof.	
random	adjective	The business owners thought a **random** survey would reveal objective consumer feedback.	

Master Student Tip

All words have a literal meaning. This is called the *denotation*. Words also have another kind of meaning, called the *connotation*. Connotation is more like the feeling people get when they hear this word. For example, the word *vomit* refers to "when you throw up." When people hear this word, they are not happy. When you learn a new word, consider both its denotation and its connotation. Doing so can be especially helpful when two words seem to have a similar meaning; sometimes one word has a positive feeling but the other word has a somewhat negative feeling. Connotation can be a powerful aid in correctly remembering a word.

EXERCISE 2 In each blank, write the correct word from the word bank. Not all the words will be used. The first one has been done for you as an example.

arbitrariness	convert	device	emerged
guarantee	mode	implicit	random

From the newest trends in business, e-marketing has (1) _emerged_ as the latest and most efficient (2) _____ of presenting new products to the general public. One of the most popular forms of e-marketing is e-mail although a great **portion** of marketing is also directed toward wireless users. The (3) _____ message in this form of advertising is that marketers should not abuse the personal space a wireless (4) _____ creates for the user. Experts caution against (5) _____ advertising and suggest ads that (6) _____ customer discounts or nonmonetary benefits as a way to (7) _____ doubtful users.

EXERCISE 3 Circle the word in parentheses that best completes each sentence.

1. The employees were (easily / randomly) chosen in order to form an objective group.

2. Most electronics firms have (converted / eliminated) to a networked computer system because it provides better internal communication.

3. The committee's decision was (arbitrary / identical) in that it did not consider the views of the consumer public.

4. The Marketing Department relied heavily on television as the primary (idea / mode) of advertising.

5. A reputable manufacturer offers a comprehensive (guarantee / uniform) with all its products in case of product defects.

6. After much discussion, an agreeable way of importing and exporting goods between the two countries (emerged / ignored).

7. Although the stuffed animal is cute and colorful, the (radical / implicit) message of child safety is conveyed by the resistant material used in the manufacturing process.

8. The portable DVD player is a popular media (device / aid) on the market today.

EXERCISE 4 Match the synonym on the left with the word on the right. Write the letters on the lines.

1. _____ changed

2. _____ not intentionally

3. _____ individually determined

4. _____ mechanism

5. _____ promised

6. _____ suggested

7. _____ way

a. arbitrarily
b. mode
c. randomly
d. implicit
e. guaranteed
f. converted
g. device

Section 2

EXERCISE 5 Read Word List 6.2. Write the part of speech and meaning for each bold vocabulary word as it is used in the corresponding example. Then verify this information with a partner or in a dictionary. The first one has been done for you as an example.

WORD LIST 6.2

Word	Example	Part of Speech & Meaning
clarity	The **clarity** of the CEO's message made it easy for the workers to understand the new production changes.	*noun; clearness*
confirms	The latest accounting report **confirms** significant economic growth for the past year.	
explicit	All sales representatives were given **explicit** orders to stop taking product requests until the defect was resolved.	
occupations	One of the most important **occupations** involved in launching a new product is the retail sales clerk.	
portion	A **portion** of that company's profits is donated to charities aiding the worldwide hunger crisis.	
stability	The **stability** of an organization is based on the effectiveness of its company leaders.	

Word	Example	Part of Speech & Meaning
transition	During a merger, the most crucial time is the **transition** of management teams.	
proportion	The amount of wage and salary spending is not in **proportion** with gross income for the fiscal year.	

Master Student Tip

Sometimes two words sound similar, and this can make learning the two words a problem. When you are learning such words, try to think of things that will help you to separate them. Two similar words from Word List 6.2 are *portion* and *proportion*. *Portion* means "a part or partial quantity of a whole," whereas *proportion* means "the balance or relationship between quantities." One way to remember these two words is to think that *portion* is "a part of something" and that the word *part* looks the more like the word *portion*. Whenever you are dealing with two similar words, check in your dictionary for more information to help distinguish them.

EXERCISE 6 Complete the following passage by writing the correct word from the word bank. The first one has been done for you as an example.

portion	clarity	occupations	explicit
confirm	transition	proportionate	stability

In 1995, a (1) _____*transition*_____ took place; the General Agreement on Tariffs and Trade (GATT) led to the founding of the World Trade Organization (WTO). The function of both organizations affects several (2) _____ and business sectors. The main objective of the WTO is to establish a (3) _____ role among worldwide producers of goods/services, importers, and exporters. A (4) _____ of the WTO's work has been in technology, telecommunication, and financial services throughout the world. The (5) _____ concern of the WTO is to oversee the (6) _____ of world trade negotiations, to (7) _____ that trade disputes are handled according to system rules, and to protect the (8) _____ that exists between the many countries composing its membership.

EXERCISE 7 Match the words on the left with the antonyms on the right. Write the letters on the lines.

1. _____ transitioning

2. _____ portion

3. _____ explicit

4. _____ stability

5. _____ confirms

6. _____ occupied

7. _____ clarity

8. _____ proportionate

a. not filled
b. indirect
c. rejects
d. not easy to understand
e. imbalanced
f. unpredictability
g. whole
h. still

Master Student Tip

   Some people say that English spelling is crazy, but do not be afraid of English spelling. Knowing something about English spelling can help you learn and then retrieve the meanings of some words. In English, words that end in -y follow specific spelling patterns. When adding verb endings, it is necessary to check the letter that precedes the -y:

- If the -y is preceded by a vowel, then simply add the -s or -ed ending (e.g., *play* becomes *plays* and *played*).
- However, if the -y is preceded by a consonant, first change the -y to -i and then add the -es or -ed ending (e.g., *try* become *tries* and *tried*).

   Knowing spelling rules such as these is important because if a word is unnecessarily hard to spell, it may also end up being hard to remember.

EXERCISE 8 Change the following words to the two indicated forms. Pay special attention to verbs that end in -*y*. The first two have been done for you as examples.

	Present tense third-person singular	**Past tense**
employ	employs	employed
clarify	clarifies	clarified
convert		
deny		
emerge		
guarantee		
modify		
confirm		
occupy		
stabilize		

Section 3

EXERCISE 9 Study Word List 6.3. Fill in the boxes in the last column with a predicted meaning for each bold vocabulary word. Then verify your predictions by consulting a dictionary. The first one has been done for you as an example.

	WORD LIST 6.3		
Word	**Part of speech**	**Example**	**Predicted Meaning**
computer	noun	Doing business by **computer** is considered typical in today's economic world.	*a machine*
compounds	verb	The toy manufacturer carefully **compounds** nontoxic plastics and color-safe fabrics when designing new products for children.	
substitution	noun	Company policy allows for either replacement or **substitution** of any returned products.	
inhibition	noun	The board chairperson showed no **inhibition** when asked about the accusations of false advertising.	
grade	noun	A higher **grade** of plastic was used to correct the manufacturing defect.	

Word	Part of speech	Example	Predicted Meaning
inevitably	adverb	The layoff of factory workers **inevitably** produced a decline in production.	
route	noun	The delivery **route** was reviewed and revised to guarantee prompter service.	

EXERCISE 10 Complete the following phrases by writing the appropriate words from Word List 6.3. The first one has been done for you as an example.

1. without ___*inhibition*___   **route**   **inhibition**

2. _____ results   substitute   inevitable

3. _____ a problem   compounding   **computer**

4. _____ a telephone call   inhibiting   routing

5. math _____   computations   **compounds**

6. mid-_____ fuel   **substitution**   **grade**

7. _____ plan   **device**   substitute

Master Student Tip

  Most words have multiple meanings. It is important to become familiar with the most common meanings a word can have rather than just the first one that appears in the dictionary entry. Read the various definitions, and then choose the ones that are the most common for your language needs.

EXERCISE 11 Use a dictionary to help you understand the multiple meanings for the words in the word bank. Then match one of the words to each definition by writing the corresponding number on the line. The first one has been done for you as an example.

1. compound	2. grade	3. route

___2___ To level off to a smooth surface

_____ To divert in a particular direction

_____ A score or judgment

_____ To increase

_____ A means of access

_____ To calculate bank account interest

_____ A way to do something

EXERCISE 12 Identify the two italicized parts in each sentence as synonyms or antonyms. The first one has been done for you as an example.

1. ___antonym___ *Computerized* mailing systems produce bulk mail faster than traditional *manual* ones used to.

2. _____ Unlike a *compounded substance*, pure gold is made up of only *one element.*

3. _____ When a *substitution* is made, one thing is removed and another is *put in its place.*

4. _____ A successful entrepreneur welcomes new ways to make money with *eagerness* and has few *inhibitions* about taking risks.

5. _____ Although the landscape architect tried to avoid a *flat* golf course design, a *graded* area had to be included for novice players.

6. _____ Whenever a product is recalled, consumers *inevitably* are concerned about return and refund procedures, so manufacturers *avoid* notifying the public until these procedures have been established.

7. _____ The announcement regarding changes in the company address was *routed* first to all managers and then *distributed* to the billing department.

Section 4

EXERCISE 13 Write six sentences using the vocabulary words from the three word lists in this chapter. Use at least two vocabulary words in each sentence, underlining the words as you go. Apply your knowledge about word forms and parts of speech to master the new words.

1. _____

_____

_____

2. _____

_____

_____

3. _____

_____

_____

4. _____

_____

_____

5. _____

_____

_____

6. _____

_____

_____

EXERCISE 14 Complete the grid by writing the correct word forms. Use your vocabulary flash cards and a dictionary to assist you if needed. The first row has been completed for you as an example.

Noun	Verb	Adjective	Adverb
computer	compute	computed	
	emerge		
occupation			
			inevitably
stability			
		explicit	
	convert		
		arbitrary	
		random	

EXERCISE 15 Complete the analogies by writing the appropriate words from the word bank. The first one has been done for you as an example.

clarity	compounded	compute
stability	transiting	substitute
proportionately	emergent	inhibits
occupied	portion	route

1. decipher :: code : _____*compute*_____ : mathematical operation

2. _____ : distribute : : evenly : allocate

3. vacant : _____ : : free : busy

4. _____ : unexpectedly : : planned : prepared

5. pure : silver : : _____ : metal

6. security : _____ : : accurateness : preciseness

7. produce : make : : exchange : _____

8. immovable : _____ : : income : expenses

9. clear : obscure : : _____ : obscurity

10. _____ : restricts : : helps : assists

11. whole : part : : complete : _____

12. _____ : path : : **device** : machine

EXERCISE 16 Complete each sentence by writing the best of the three word choices. The first one has been done for you as an example.

1. The palm pilot is a _____ *device* _____ that helps organize appointments and business contact information.

   device   interval   scheme

2. The _____ assumption was that a merger was the only solution to the financial crisis.

   successful   implicit   accompanied

3. The friendly _____ of negotiation facilitated the signing of a contract for future expansion.

   ministry   mode   inspection

4. For an additional twenty dollars, the company will _____ delivery within forty-eight hours.

   guarantee   minimize   ignore

5. Employment promotions require completion of a "_____ Change Request" form that has been signed by both the employee and her or his immediate supervisor.

   Sphere   Grade   Citation

6. We received a written _____ of our recent order for replacement parts.

   exposure   confirmation   integration

7. During this _____ stage, all franchises are requested to continue the same high-quality service to their clients.

   transitory   identical   finite

8. A _____ of the investment income has been placed in a reserve account for research on customer needs.

   theory   portion   statistic

9. Various _____ are available to individuals wanting to start their own small businesses.

   domains   routes   couples

10. Several European businessowners thought the monetary
_____ to euros caused consumers to change their
spending habits.

phenomenon   conversion   ideology

11. Financial advisers recommend choosing _____
between high-risk and more conservative investment options.

proportionately   somewhat   crucially

12. Unpaid tax bills _____ the company's financial
problems of overspending and declining sales.

liberated   compounded   assigned

13. The union leader _____ stated that no workers
would agree to return to the job site until the human resource disputes
had been settled.

environmentally   explicitly   beneficially

14. The winners of the sweepstakes drawing were _____
selected and notified in person.

domestically   randomly   uniformly

15. An _____ economy directly affects interest rates and
unemployment statistics.

immature   unstable   rational

W E B   P O W E R

You will find additional exercises related to the content
in this chapter at **http://esl.college.hmco.com/students.**